Adapted Tests

Motion, Forces, and Energy

PRENTICE HALL Science Explorer

PEARSON

Prentice Hall

Boston, Massachusetts
Upper Saddle River, New Jersey

ISBN 0-13-166588-X
9 10   09

Motion, Forces, and Energy

Motion

Multiple Choice

Write the letter of the correct answer on the line at the left.

_____ 1. The SI unit for length is
   a. meter.
   b. meters per second.
   c. slope.

_____ 2. The formula for speed is
   a. distance ÷ time.
   b. distance + time.
   c. distance × time.

_____ 3. A rider finishes a 10-km bicycle trip in 2 hours. The average speed of the rider is
   a. 20 km/hr.
   b. 10 km/hr.
   c. 5 km/hr.

_____ 4. A runner starts a 5-km race at 10:15 a.m. She finishes at 10:45 a.m. With this information you can calculate the runner's
   a. velocity.
   b. average speed.
   c. acceleration.

_____ 5. A velocity tells
   a. only speed.
   b. only direction.
   c. speed and direction.

_____ 6. Earth's plates
   a. move slowly.
   b. move quickly.
   c. do not move at all.

_____ 7. What formula can be used to find the distance that one of Earth's plates moves in a certain amount of time?
   a. Distance = Speed ÷ Time
   b. Distance = Speed × Time
   c. Distance = Speed + Time

Motion

_____ 8. A car traveling at 25 m/s speeds up to 30 m/s over a period of 5 seconds. The average acceleration of the car is
  a. 1 m/s^2.
  b. 5 m/s^2.
  c. 25 m/s^2.

_____ 9. To find an object's acceleration, you need to know its starting speed, its ending speed, and
  a. velocity.
  b. time.
  c. distance.

_____ 10. A flat line on speed-versus-time graph shows an object that is
  a. not accelerating.
  b. accelerating quickly.
  c. slowing down.

Completion

Read each word in the box. In each sentence below, fill in the correct word or words. Not all words will be used.

slope	plate tectonics	reference point
acceleration	velocity	average speed

11. An object is in motion if it is moving relative to a(an)

 _____.

12. Total distance traveled divided by the total time equals

 _____.

13. The _____ of a line on a motion graph tells the rate of change.

14. The theory of _____ describes the motion of Earth's plates.

15. Increasing speed, decreasing speed, and changing direction are all _____.

Motion

True or False

If a statement is true, write true. *If it is false, write* false.

_____ **16.** An object is in motion if its distance from a reference point is changing.

_____ **17.** To describe a velocity you need to know speed and direction.

_____ **18.** If you know the instantaneous speed of an object, you also know its average speed.

_____ **19.** Earth's plates move due to ocean currents.

_____ **20.** An object cannot be accelerating if it is changing direction.

Using Science Skills

Use the graph below to answer questions 21, 22, and 23.

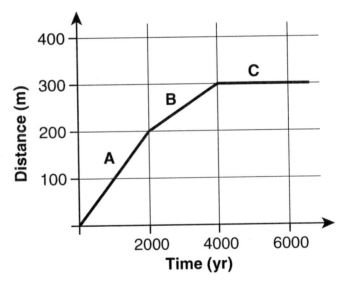

Motion of an Imaginary Continent

_____ **21. Interpreting Graphs** Which part of the line shows a time when the continent was not moving?

    a. A

    b. B

    c. C

_____ **22. Interpreting Graphs** Which part of the line shows a time when the continent had the greatest acceleration?

    a. A

    b. B

    c. C

_____ **23. Interpreting Graphs** How far did the continent move in the first 2000 years?

    a. 100 m

    b. 200 m

    c. 300 m

Using Science Skills

The diagram below shows the acceleration of an airplane. Use the diagram to answer questions 24 and 25.

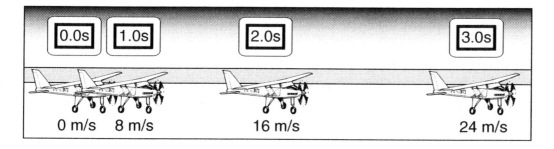

_____ **24. Calculating** What is this object's acceleration during the 3 seconds of motion?

    a. 3 m/s^2

    b. 8 m/s^2

    c. 24 m/s^2

_____ **25. Interpreting Diagrams** During which time period did the airplane travel the least distance?

    a. between 0.0 s and 1.0 s

    b. between 1.0 s and 2.0 s

    c. between 2.0 s and 3.0 s

Forces

Multiple Choice

Write the letter of the correct answer on the line at the left.

_____ 1. A force is described by
  a. its strength only.
  b. its direction only.
  c. its strength and direction.

_____ 2. What is the SI unit for force?
  a. meter
  b. meters per second
  c. newton

_____ 3. When the forces acting on an object are balanced, the net force on the object is
  a. less than 0.
  b. exactly 0.
  c. more than 0.

_____ 4. Friction acts
  a. in the same direction as motion.
  b. only on objects that are not in motion.
  c. in the opposite direction as motion.

_____ 5. The friction on an object moving through water or air is
  a. rolling friction.
  b. sliding friction.
  c. fluid friction.

_____ 6. The amount of gravity between two objects depends on their masses and the
  a. distance between them.
  b. friction between them.
  c. total velocity of the objects.

_____ 7. The force of gravity on an object is known as its
  a. acceleration.
  b. mass.
  c. weight.

Forces

_____ 8. Air resistance acts in what direction on a falling object?
   a. upward
   b. sideways
   c. downward

_____ 9. A(An) _____causes an object's motion to change.
   a. inertia
   b. unbalanced force
   c. balanced force

_____ 10. Newton's third law says that for every action there is an equal and opposite reaction. This law says that forces
   a. do not act on moving objects.
   b. come in pairs.
   c. act only in the opposite direction of motion.

Completion

Read each word in the box. In each sentence below, fill in the correct word or words. Not all words will be used.

mass	weight	force	velocity	free fall	static

11. A push or a pull is a _____.

12. Friction between two objects that are not moving is _____ friction.

13. If gravity is the only force acting on an object, the object is in _____.

14. The measure of the amount of matter in an object is the object's _____.

15. The momentum of an object depends on its mass and its _____.

True or False

If a statement is true, write true. *If it is false, write* false.

_____ 16. Unbalanced forces change an object's motion.

_____ 17. Friction causes moving objects to speed up.

Forces

_____ 18. The force of gravity between objects gets stronger as the objects move further apart.

_____ 19. The inertia of an object depends on its mass.

_____ 20. A centripetal force is the force that keeps a satellite in orbit.

Using Science Skills

The diagram below shows two balls. Use the diagram to answer questions 21, 22, and 23.

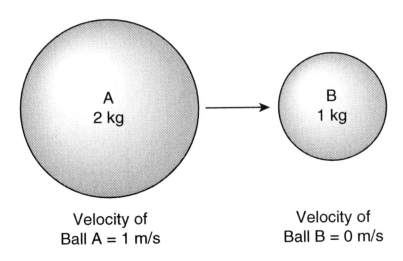

Velocity of
Ball A = 1 m/s

Velocity of
Ball B = 0 m/s

_____ 21. **Calculating** The momentum of an object is its mass times its velocity. What is the momentum of Ball A?

  a. 1 kg·m/s

  b. 2 kg·m/s

  c. 3 kg·m/s

_____ 22. **Calculating** What is the momentum of Ball B?

  a. 0 kg·m/s

  b. 1 kg·m/s

  c. 10 kg·m/s

_____ 23. **Applying Concepts** If Ball A hits Ball B, what will the total momentum of the two balls be after the collision?

  a. 1 kg·m/s

  b. 2 kg·m/s

  c. 3 kg·m/s

Name _____ Date _____ Class _____

Forces

Using Science Skills

Use the graph below to answer questions 24 and 25.

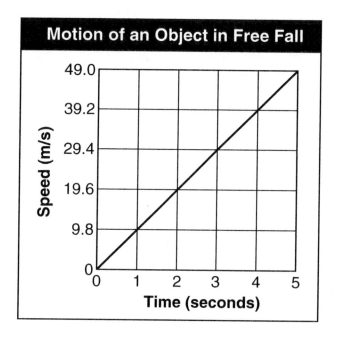

Motion of an Object in Free Fall

_____ **24. Interpreting Graphs** What is the object's speed at 3 seconds?

    a. 19.6 m/s

    b. 29.4 m/s

    c. 39.2 m/s

_____ **25. Applying Concepts** This graph shows an object in free fall. What is the only force acting on this object?

    a. air resistance

    b. gravity

    c. terminal velocity

Forces in Fluids

Forces in Fluids

Multiple Choice

Write the letter of the correct answer on the line at the left.

_____ 1. What is the SI unit for pressure?
  a. pascal (Pa)
  b. newton (N)
  c. kilogram (kg)

_____ 2. Pressure is
  a. force $\times$ area.
  b. force $\div$ area.
  c. force + area.

_____ 3. At higher elevations, there is _____ air pressure.
  a. the same
  b. greater
  c. less

_____ 4. As a diver moves deeper in the water, the fluid pressure is
  a. the same.
  b. greater.
  c. less.

_____ 5. Objects in water feel lighter because of the
  a. buoyant force.
  b. air pressure.
  c. temperature.

_____ 6. An object sinks in a bucket of water. The object's density is
  a. less than water's density.
  b. the same as water's density.
  c. greater than water's density.

_____ 7. A force on a confined fluid changes the pressure all through the fluid. This is
  a. Pascal's principle.
  b. Archimedes' principle.
  c. Bernoulli's principle.

_____ 8. A hydraulic system uses fluid to
  a. cause acceleration.
  b. decrease air pressure.
  c. multiply force.

Forces in Fluids

_____ 9. As the speed of a moving fluid increases, the fluid pressure
    a. decreases.
    b. stays the same.
    c. increases.

_____ 10. What force pushes up on an airplane wing as it moves through the air?
    a. gravity
    b. lift
    c. air resistance

Completion

Read each word in the box. In each sentence below, fill in the correct word or words. Not all words will be used.

mass	Bernoulli's principle	force
air pressure	gravity	hydraulic device

11. Pressure tells how much _____ is on an area.

12. The pressure exerted by Earth's atmosphere is

_____ .

13. The density of an object is its _____ divided by its volume.

14. A(An) _____ uses fluid to transmit a force.

15. The flow of smoke up a chimney is partly explained by

_____ .

True or False

If a statement is true, write true. *If it is false, write* false.

_____ **16.** Water pressure increases as depth increases.

_____ **17.** Air pressure is measured using a barometer.

_____ **18.** The buoyant force acts in a downward direction.

_____ **19.** The buoyant force on an object is equal to the weight of the fluid the object displaces.

_____ **20.** Archimedes' principle explains how an airplane flies.

Forces in Fluids

Forces in Fluids

Using Science Skills

Use the diagram below to answer questions 21 and 22.

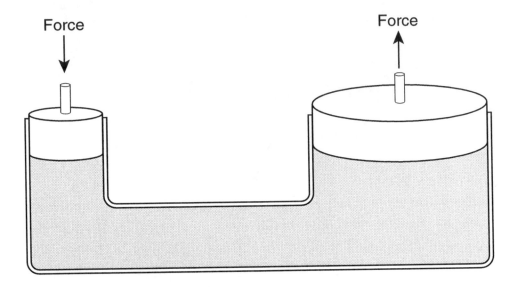

_____ **21. Classifying** This device is a

    a. barometer.

    b. hydraulic system.

    c. buoyant force.

_____ **22. Applying Concepts** This device uses fluid to multiply force. Which principle explains why this device works?

    a. Pascal's principle

    b. Archimedes' principle

    c. Bernoulli's principle

Forces in Fluids

Using Science Skills

Use the diagram below to answer questions 23, 24, and 25.

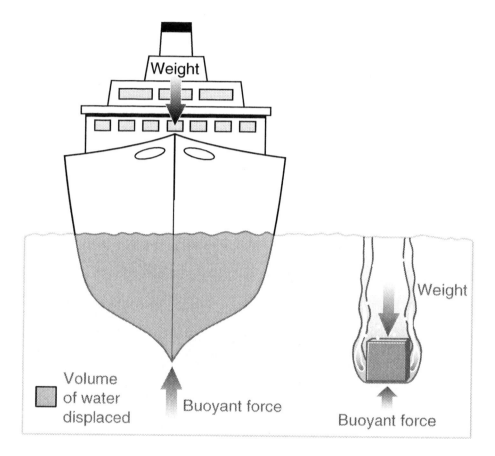

_____ 23. **Interpreting Diagrams** The ship and the steel block have the same weight. Why does the ship float while the steel block sinks?

    a. The ship displaces more water.

    b. There is less gravity on the ship.

    c. There is no air pressure on the ship.

_____ 24. **Applying Concepts** Which principle explains why the ship floats and the steel block sinks?

    a. Pascal's principle

    b. Archimedes' principle

    c. Bernoulli's principle

_____ 25. **Applying Concepts** What does the buoyant force on each object in the diagram equal?

    a. the weight of the object

    b. the weight of the water displaced by the object

    c. the weight of the air pressing down on the object

Work and Machines

Multiple Choice

Write the letter of the correct answer on the line at the left.

_____ 1. Work equals
   a. force × distance.
   b. force − distance.
   c. force + distance.

_____ 2. The unit of work is the
   a. watt.
   b. newton.
   c. joule.

_____ 3. Power is the amount of
   a. work done per unit of time.
   b. force on a certain area.
   c. pressure in a volume of liquid.

_____ 4. The unit for power is the
   a. joule.
   b. meter per second.
   c. watt.

_____ 5. A machine cannot change the
   a. direction of the input force.
   b. amount of work needed to do a task.
   c. distance over which a force is applied.

_____ 6. The force you apply to a machine is the
   a. input force.
   b. output force.
   c. efficiency.

_____ 7. The efficiency of all real machines is
   a. greater than 100%.
   b. equal to 100%.
   c. less than 100%.

_____ 8. The fixed point that a lever rotates around is called the
   a. fulcrum.
   b. input force.
   c. wedge.

Work and Machines

___ 9. A screwdriver is an example of a simple machine called a
    a. pulley.
    b. screw.
    c. wheel and axle.

___ 10. Your front teeth are
    a. wedges.
    b. levers.
    c. compound machines.

Completion

Read each word in the box. In each sentence below, fill in the correct word or words. Not all words will be used.

move	efficiency	inclined plane
wedge	screw	pulley

11. In order to do work on an object, the object must
_____ as a result of your force.

12. A machine's _____ compares the input
work to the output work.

13. An inclined plane wrapped in a circle is a(an)
_____.

14. A rope wrapped around a grooved wheel is a(an)
_____.

15. A ramp is an example of a(an) _____.

True or False

If a statement is true, write true. *If it is false, write* false.

_____ 16. All forces do work.

_____ 17. Power is how quickly work is done.

_____ 18. A machine makes work easier.

_____ 19. A pulley can change the direction of the input force.

_____ 20. Simple machines are made up of compound machines.

Work and Machines

Using Science Skills

Use the diagram below to answer questions 21 and 22.

Jill

F = 40 N

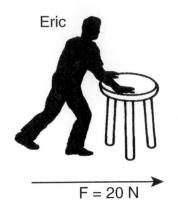

Eric

F = 20 N

_____ **21. Applying Concepts** Jill pushes the table with a force of 40 newtons. If the table does not move,

    a. no force was acting on the table.

    b. no work was done on the table.

    c. gravity did not act on the table.

_____ **22. Calculating** Work = Force × Distance. If Eric moved the stool 3 meters, how much work did he perform?

    a. 20 joules

    b. 23 joules

    c. 60 joules

Work and Machines

Using Science Skills

Use the picture below to answer questions 23, 24, and 25.

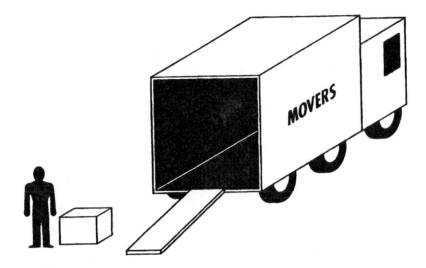

_____ 23. **Interpreting Diagrams** What kind of simple machine is the ramp in this picture?

a. pulley

b. lever

c. inclined plane

_____ 24. **Applying Concepts** How does the ramp make work easier?

a. It increases force.

b. It decreases work.

c. It changes the distance of a force.

_____ 25. **Applying Concepts** When the mover pushes the box up the ramp, there is friction between the box and the ramp. What is the efficiency of this ramp?

a. greater than 100%

b. exactly 100%

c. less than 100%

Energy

Multiple Choice

Write the letter of the correct answer on the line at the left.

_____ 1. Potential energy is energy
    a. that is stored.
    b. of distance.
    c. of motion.

_____ 2. Kinetic energy depends on
    a. only velocity.
    b. mass and velocity.
    c. height and mass.

_____ 3. The energy in springs and rubber bands is
    a. elastic potential energy.
    b. gravitational potential energy.
    c. thermal energy.

_____ 4. A ball thrown straight up in the air has the most potential energy
    a. at its lowest point.
    b. halfway to its greatest height.
    c. at its highest point.

_____ 5. An object's mechanical energy is its
    a. potential energy + kinetic energy.
    b. kinetic energy − potential energy.
    c. potential energy × kinetic energy.

_____ 6. The form of energy stored in the bonds between atoms and molecules is
    a. electromagnetic energy.
    b. chemical energy.
    c. electrical energy.

_____ 7. The sunlight that reaches Earth is one kind of
    a. electromagnetic energy.
    b. chemical energy.
    c. electrical energy.

Energy

_____ 8. A toaster changes electrical energy to thermal energy. This is a(an)

　　a. energy conservation.

　　b. fossil fuel.

　　c. energy transformation.

_____ 9. When energy changes form,

　　a. energy is lost.

　　b. energy is created.

　　c. energy is not lost or created.

_____ 10. Fossil fuels store

　　a. chemical energy.

　　b. mechanical energy.

　　c. electrical energy.

Completion

Read each word in the box. In each sentence below, fill in one of the words. Not all words will be used.

potential	power	kinetic
combustion	mechanical	chemical

11. A moving object has _____ energy.

12. A measure of how much energy is transferred in a unit of time is

_____.

13. Energy due to an object's position and motion is its

_____ energy.

14. The energy in fossil fuels is released during

_____.

15. Living plants convert electromagnetic energy to

_____ energy.

True or False

If a statement is true, write true. *If it is false, write* false.

_____ **16.** Work is the transfer of energy.

_____ **17.** Potential energy that depends on height is elastic potential energy.

Energy

_____ **18.** A pendulum has the most kinetic energy at the top of its swing.

_____ **19.** The law of conservation of energy states that some energy is lost when energy changes forms.

_____ **20.** Fossil fuels form over a short period of time.

Using Science Skills

Use the picture below to answer questions 21, 22, and 23.

____ **21. Interpreting Diagrams** At what point does the ball have the most potential energy?

    a. 1

    b. 3

    c. 4

____ **22. Interpreting Diagrams** At what point does the ball have the most kinetic energy?

    a. 1

    b. 2

    c. 3

____ **23. Applying Concepts** What happens as the ball moves from position 1 to position 3?

    a. Energy is created.

    b. Energy is lost.

    c. Energy changes forms.

Name _____ Date _____ Class _____

Energy

Using Science Skills

Use the diagram below to answer questions 24 and 25.

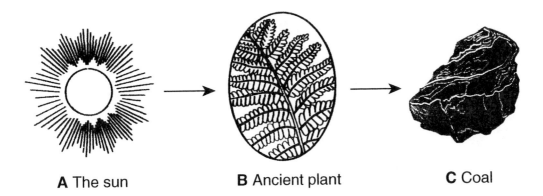

A The sun   **B** Ancient plant   **C** Coal

_____ 24. **Interpreting Diagrams** What energy transformation happens at Step B?
   a. electromagnetic energy to chemical energy
   b. thermal energy to electromagnetic energy
   c. chemical energy to electromagnetic energy

_____ 25. **Applying Concepts** Coal is an example of what kind of fuel?
   a. thermal fuel
   b. fossil fuel
   c. electrical fuel

Name _____ Date _____ Class _____

Thermal Energy and Heat

Multiple Choice

Write the letter of the correct answer on the line at the left.

_____ 1. On which temperature scale does water boil at 100 degrees?
   a. Fahrenheit
   b. Celsius
   c. Kelvin

_____ 2. Temperature is a measure of the average _____ of each particle in an object.
   a. kinetic energy
   b. heat
   c. potential energy

_____ 3. Heat is
   a. moving thermal energy.
   b. moving potential energy.
   c. moving kinetic energy.

_____ 4. Heat transfer in a moving fluid is
   a. radiation.
   b. conduction.
   c. convection.

_____ 5. Heat moves
   a. in all directions.
   b. from cooler objects to warmer objects.
   c. from warmer objects to cooler objects.

_____ 6. A winter coat is made of materials that are good
   a. conductors.
   b. refrigerants.
   c. insulators.

_____ 7. Which state of matter has particles that move the most?
   a. solid
   b. liquid
   c. gas

_____ 8. The change of state from a liquid to a solid is
   a. melting.
   b. vaporization.
   c. freezing.

_____ 9. A device that changes thermal energy to mechanical energy is a
  a. refrigerant.
  b. cooling system.
  c. heat engine.

_____ 10. An object usually gets _____ when its temperature increases.
  a. bigger
  b. colder
  c. smaller

Completion

Read each word in the box. In each sentence below, fill in the correct word or words. Not all words will be used.

solids	convection	cooling system
thermal	radiation	vaporization

11. The total energy in all of the particles in a substance is _____ energy.

12. The transfer of energy by electromagnetic waves is _____.

13. A change of state from a liquid to a gas is _____.

14. The particles in _____ are packed in fixed positions.

15. A device that moves thermal energy from a cool area to a warm area is a _____.

True or False

If a statement is true, write true. *If it is false, write* false.

_____ 16. Water freezes at 0° Fahrenheit.

_____ 17. Heat is the transfer of thermal energy.

_____ 18. A conductor does not allow heat to move easily.

Thermal Energy and Heat

_____ **19.** The particles in a gas move quickly.

_____ **20.** Heat engines convert mechanical energy to chemical energy.

Using Science Skills

The picture below shows a pan of water on a stove. Use the picture to answer questions 21, 22, and 23.

____ **21. Interpreting Diagrams** What temperature scale does this thermometer use?
  a. Celsius
  b. Kelvin
  c. Fahrenheit

____ **22. Interpreting Diagrams** What change of state is happening?
  a. melting
  b. boiling
  c. freezing

____ **23. Applying Concepts** The handle of this pot is cool, even though it is on a hot stove. What kind of material was used to make the pot's handle?
  a. conductor
  b. thermometer
  c. insulator

Name _____ Date _____ Class _____

Thermal Energy and Heat

Using Science Skills

The picture below shows a fireplace. Use the picture to answer questions 24 and 25.

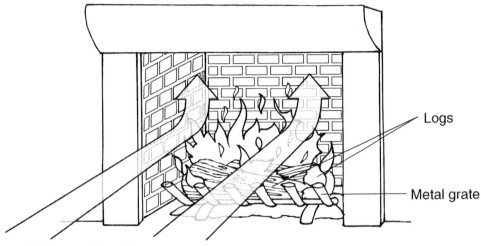

Logs

Metal grate

Air flow up the chimney

_____ 24. **Interpreting Diagrams** The air moving up the chimney transfers heat in what way?

  a. radiation

  b. convection

  c. conduction

_____ 25. **Interpreting Diagrams** The metal grate under the logs is touching the hot logs. It is heated by

  a. conduction.

  b. convection.

  c. radiation.

Name _____ Date _____ Class _____

Motion, Forces, and Energy

Multiple Choice

Write the letter of the correct answer on the line at the left.

_____ 1. The steepness of a line on a motion graph is called its
   a. direction.
   b. velocity.
   c. slope.

_____ 2. An object's speed at a moment in time is its
   a. average speed.
   b. velocity.
   c. instantaneous speed.

_____ 3. _____ do not change an object's motion.
   a. Unbalanced forces
   b. Balanced forces
   c. Newtons

_____ 4. Gravity is a force that pulls moving objects
   a. upward.
   b. downward.
   c. sideways.

_____ 5. If you squeeze one end of a closed tube of toothpaste, the pressure at the other end of the tube
   a. increases.
   b. decreases.
   c. stays the same.

_____ 6. Air pressure is measured using a
   a. thermometer.
   b. barometer.
   c. conductor.

_____ 7. A simple machine that is a flat, sloped surface is a(an)
   a. inclined plane.
   b. pulley.
   c. lever.

_____ 8. What is a compound machine?
   a. a machine that changes the work needed to do a task
   b. a machine made up of simple machines
   c. a machine used to weigh objects

_____ 9. The formula for gravitational potential energy is
   a. weight × height.
   b. mass × weight.
   c. velocity × mass.

_____ 10. Thermal energy is
   a. the total energy in the particles of an object.
   b. the energy of electrical charges.
   c. the energy in the bonds of atoms and molecules.

Completion

Read each word in the box. In each sentence below, fill in the correct word or words. Not all words will be used.

dense	centripetal force	conductors
insulators	velocity	Kelvin

11. To find an object's momentum you need to know its mass and
   _____.

12. A _____ keeps satellites in orbit.

13. An object that is more _____ than water will sink in water.

14. The three temperature scales are Fahrenheit, Celsius, and
   _____.

15. Materials like wood that do not conduct heat well are called
   _____.

True or False

If a statement is true, write true. *If it is false, write* false.

_____ 16. The SI unit of length is the pascal.

_____ 17. For every action force there is an equal and opposite reaction force.

_____ 18. The buoyant force pushes upward on objects in fluids.

_____ 19. Hydraulic systems transmit velocity.

_____ 20. All fuels have potential energy.

Name _____ Date _____ Class _____

Motion, Forces, and Energy

Using Science Skills

The picture below shows a wet road in a desert. Use the picture to answer questions 21, 22, and 23.

_____ 21. **Interpreting Diagrams** What change of state is happening in this picture?

   a. condensation

   b. vaporization

   c. melting

_____ 22. **Classifying** What form of energy is the sun's light?

   a. chemical

   b. electromagnetic

   c. electrical

_____ 23. **Applying Concepts** What energy transformation is happening in the cacti plants in the picture?

   a. thermal energy to chemical energy

   b. chemical energy to electrical energy

   c. electromagnetic energy to chemical energy

Motion, Forces, and Energy

Using Science Skills

Use the graph below to answer questions 24 and 25.

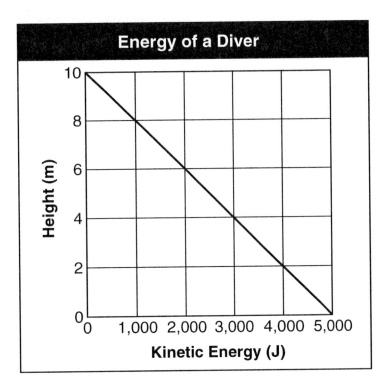

_____ 24. **Interpreting Graphs** This graph shows the kinetic energy of a diver after she dove from a high platform. As the diver moves downward, what happens to her kinetic energy?

    a. It increases.

    b. It decreases.

    c. It stays the same.

_____ 25. **Applying Concepts** As the diver's kinetic energy increases, what happens to her mechanical energy?

    a. It increases.

    b. It decreases.

    c. It stays the same.

Chapter 1, Motion

1. a
2. a
3. c
4. b
5. c
6. a
7. b
8. a
9. b
10. a
11. reference point
12. average speed
13. slope
14. plate tectonics
15. acceleration
16. true
17. true
18. false
19. false
20. false
21. c
22. a
23. b
24. b
25. a

Chapter 2, Forces

1. c
2. c
3. b
4. c
5. c
6. a
7. c
8. a
9. b
10. b
11. force
12. static
13. free fall
14. mass
15. velocity
16. true
17. false
18. false
19. true
20. true
21. b
22. a
23. b
24. b
25. b

Chapter 3, Forces in Fluids

1. a
2. b
3. c
4. b
5. a
6. c
7. a
8. c
9. a
10. b
11. force
12. air pressure
13. mass
14. hydraulic device
15. Bernoulli's principle
16. true
17. true
18. false
19. true
20. false
21. b
22. a
23. a
24. b
25. b

Chapter 4, Work and Machines

1. a
2. c
3. a
4. c
5. b
6. a
7. c
8. a
9. c
10. a
11. move
12. efficiency
13. screw
14. pulley
15. inclined plane
16. false
17. true
18. true
19. true
20. false
21. b
22. c
23. c
24. c
25. c

Chapter 5, Energy

1. a
2. b
3. a
4. c
5. a
6. b
7. a
8. c
9. c
10. a
11. kinetic
12. power
13. mechanical
14. combustion
15. chemical
16. true
17. false
18. false
19. false
20. false
21. b
22. b
23. c
24. a
25. b

Chapter 6, Thermal Energy and Heat

1. b
2. a
3. a
4. c
5. c
6. c
7. c
8. c
9. c
10. a
11. thermal
12. radiation
13. vaporization
14. solids
15. cooling system
16. false
17. true
18. false
19. true
20. false
21. a
22. b
23. c
24. b
25. a

Book Test, Motion, Forces and Energy

1. c
2. c
3. b
4. b
5. a
6. b
7. a
8. b
9. a
10. a
11. velocity
12. centripetal force
13. dense
14. Kelvin
15. insulators
16. false
17. true
18. true
19. false
20. true
21. b
22. b
23. c
24. a
25. c